LINES IN MY HEAD

SWETA SINGH

Copyright © Sweta Singh
All Rights Reserved.

*To my parents…who always believed in me and made me what
I am today….*

I will love you forever with all dedication

Contents

Acknowledgements

Acknowledgment

I wish to express my heartfelt gratitude to my family, my friends and all my respected teachers. This book could not have been completed without the constant support of these gems in my life. You all are my biggest fan, my biggest support and I will truly and always be dedicated and soulfully devoted towards you all.

I would also like to acknowledge the extraordinary debt I owe to the writers who told me such wise things about poetry writing over the years.

1. Table of Contents

2. When I Miss You

There are so many times in our lives, when we are away from our loved ones, when there's nothing but their memories that surround us and we simply recall their touch and how mazing their presence is…It was a weekend night when I was sitting alone and wasn't able to think of anything else but of how blessed I am for having such amazing people in my life… who love me with all my imperfections, who have accepted me despite all my mistakes, and who push me towards my growth always. However, in spite of so many people and their memories we feel lonely… not really because we don't have anyone but because we are unable to find ourselves…

When I Miss You…

Beneath the moon
Under the star
These winds are making me realise you are so far
I sat alone for meditation
But remembered my peace is in you
Even with everyone, I am in isolation
The moments to rejoice are few...
The soft wind reminds me of you
Your hands and your touch

The breeze is whispering in my ears
The time is coming that will end all my fears...

• 3 •

3. When the Rain Poured Your Love

The time I wrote this poem, was when I was sitting alone in a chair at night, on terrace, it was hailing that night and the slow wind was preventing me from getting watery, but there was only one thought that was going in my mind or I should say only one person, and that is when I couldn't resist but write…

<u>When the rain Poured your love…</u>

These droplets are messengers from you
Delivering me your hugs and kisses
They know each moment we are together is new
And so they serve me your love giving me infinite blisses...
You are and will always be my love
Forever with all devotion to you I'll serve
All the feelings that I have for you are so pure
You earned them all, this is for sure
I love you and will always till my last breath
Will always lay roses in our happiness bed
Will take away all the thorns
Will never let anything touch you that make you mourn
You are the definition of what I know as love

You are my angel, my innocent dove
You are the reason I look forward to each day ahead
Without you it's only tears that I shred...

4. Waiting For You

Waiting… what is waiting? Is it just sitting for someone and wanting the to arrive soon? Or something more? Can't we wait for someone even after being with them? Can't we expect someone to come back to being what they were?... Well we call come to this situation at some point of time, where we desperately wish for someone to return…may it be physically or in an abstract manner, later or sooner this happens and we retain our peace of mind and attain some different level of happiness and self-satisfaction….

Waiting for you…

There's a que of emotions like a train
No one can understand my pain
The feeling of Missing you so bad
But we'll meet soon, I'm glad
Imagining I'm going to see you soon
Gives me Goosebumps each time
The moment we meet will be a full moon
And everything will rhyme
I'll be holding you close and safe
Will keep you in place with no escape
Will give you all the love you deserve

With all my passion to you I'll serve
I can't wait to have you beside me again
To hold the hands that relieves all my pain
To keep my head on your shoulders
To again pour my mood swings on your moulders
Emotions are many, words are less
Each time without you, I am a mess
You are the one who complete me so...
Please come fast, and I'll never let you go...

5. Life

Life, One of the most misunderstood word. It is more than just these four letters, each one of us has a different definition of life and none can be considered and untrue or wrong, we define such huge words as per the experiences we have, for instance, people who are well to do define life as amazing and satisfying, whereas people having not basic amenities in life define life as cruel and unfulfilling… though life has nothing to do with it…life is the same for all, it only differs in its span for every individual and what next it brings to every being…

<u>*LIFE*</u>

I always knew life is beautiful,
full of challenge and surprise....
every moment is cheerful,
if started with a smile, on every sun rise.....
life is unpredictable,
no one knows what's next to come......
not all things that come to us are acceptable,
but to accept all are some......
life is amazing,

it brings us close to a number of friends......
people whom we would have been chasing,
become so dear, that relation never ends...
life is what we want it to be,
a bit bitter, a bit sweet....
it all depends how we see,
with sorrow how we cheat......
it's not always easy to smile,
but it's not even that hard too......
just sit and think for a while,
shout loud....life I'm coming towards you....

6. Last Time

As a writer I always keep in mind the emotions that I am meaning is going to flow through my words, the feelings, the different interpretations and the various impacts that my works are going to have on my readers. However, we all are unique in our ways and can chalk out different meanings of different words keeping aside their literal ones. When I wrote *Last Time* I was in a completely different stage of my life, one in which we all come across…and it goes like….

Last Time…

Last time what I wrote was what I felt
those words made some people melt..
they related to some….while some may differ….
but that's what life is all about.. we don't always get what we
prefer……
last time what I spoke was what I saw..
those feelings were hard and very raw..
I know I was rude and a bit arrogant….
but that's how I had to express…how it was meant….
last time when I smiled…
the reason was small and a bit mild…
I got a mare balloon…that bought a smile to my face…

the happiness that nothing can give…nor a royal place…

last time when I cried..

the reason was something…but to stop I tried…

I got hurt from within…that broke me all

but I tried to rise…after a deep fall

last time when I talked…

those people didn't listen n they walked…..

I didn't stop speaking….because I had a wish….

I knew god will gift me friends so beautiful who are reading

this…….

7. The Past

Past…this is really a haunting word… for a lot of you it would be a mesmerizing one but I can guaranty you for out of ten people eight will always say 'They don't want to talk about it.' Our past holds so much of ourselves, our lives, our good-bad experiences, our learnings from those experiences and our growth those experiences caused. Though no-one in the world can be defined by their past, some people grow to be a king and some to be a beggar, some people learn from their past and some wants to become a topic of past… Choice is ours…

<u>The Past</u>

I remember how wished for my dreams to come true,
always wondered…will something happen that's new?
I remember when I was a child..
when worries were few and wounds were mild….

the way my father used to carry me on his shoulders,
just to make me see the beautiful world….
he made me aware…one day I'll grow older,
in this crowd of people ill b whirled…

the way my mother used to pamper me always,
saved me from everything that may hurt me.....
I am an angel to her she says...
but it's my goddess in her, that I see....

the way my sister used to irritate me...
with her annoying talks and prank,
but still used to care and look after me...
that brought her to the top rank.....

I remember how things used to be
its still the same, but differently I see...

8. A New Place

Shifting to a new place, all alone all by ourselves is at some point everyone's dream…to enjoy their freedom, to explore their capabilities, to take charge of their lives…but moving out of the comfort nest built by our families to a barren land in search of building your own empire… is not an easy task…the world outside takes a lot from you to give you little and that's when you realize….

A New Place

Went to new places
was so happy…so excited…
But what I found was not expected
people are weird…with their unhappy faces….

Everyone's busy at there work and life
no time for friends, family or wife..
They all want to run faster than time..
putting money on the prime

Here's no one is real...everyone's fake
no one gives a smile to each other....
Not even for humanity sake....
no one's here to bother......

The importance of family is felt now
the feeling of being with them is soo WOW
They are always with us at all stages....
when we laugh, we cry....at every phase

I felt it now that the bigger the town
the more busy the people are
The smaller the town
the more social the people are...
At last the only thing that remains is..
The love of family, the care of siblings...
The fun of friends......
That's what with life should end...........

9. A New Feeling

Feelings…what are feelings? Is it just: a physical or emotional experience or just a sensation of pain, warmth or cold, or something more than that?, for me 'feelings' is a completely abstract idea. Sometimes what we cannot express, what we experience and something that makes us speechless are all our feelings. Some of you will relate with me and some may differ, its just because some of you may feel what I wished to convey and some me not, but at the end what remains is our feelings…

A New Feeling

I always try hard but I fail
I always want to stay but I sail
There's always a feeling of being lost
To be trusted, paying a high cost

There's always a feeling of being alone
To find a safe place where no one has gone
There's always an emptiness that surrounds me
It's too dark that nothing I can see

I always wish to end it forever

Seeing my mum. I wish to do it never
I always try to do something I always wished to
To support the same I find few

When I am right, there's someone always to ignore
When I am wrong, there's everyone to blame

I wonder when all this will end
I wonder whether I will able to mend
Ever these things will change
Will I come out of this cage?

Ever I will make my father trust me
Ever with faith at me he'll see
Ever he'll cheer my joy
Ever he will realize I am not a toy

That will hear everything and stay quite
It's what protest when it's not right
It's important to understand
People can change if given a chance
It's not good to make their image at a glance…..

10. Sorry

Sorry… the most used and misused word after 'I Love You'. People think they are commit any crime and by expressing how sorry they are for the same they can get away with its aftermaths. But this is not really that happens in life. As mentioned in *Mahabharata* Lord Krishna forgave ninety-nine abusive words of Shishupal but on the hundredth abusive word, Lord Krishna beheaded him with his Sudershan Chakra. The God Almighty, who is so generous towards all his beings be it in a human or non-human form, does not forgive after a significance span of time, then we are human beings. However, God has given the ample amount of sensibility to each being to differentiate between good and bad deeds and act accordingly… Rest is all your choice…

<u>Sorry</u>

Feeling so lonely
So dull….
There's always a feeling of guilt
And understanding it is null

All that happens to me, is done by me
All that I face
Is chosen by me…and it feels like
Only I can see….

No one will ever forgive me
They say that they will…
But there's always a culprit in me that they see
And that is what tries me to kill..

I always wanted to live my life the way I always wanted too
But, every time I did it
The happiness I got was few…
With people backed with taunts and criticism….
And driving my life zig zag n no rhythm….

I am ending up everting with myself….
Coz this will never end….
I am weak not too strong to bear it all always…
Neither to carry this guilt shelf..
I AM SORRY FOR EVERTHING….
Is only left to say…

11. A Small Wish

Wishes…unexplainable and undeniable. Even the world-wide accepted definition of 'Wish' does not justify what wishes are. Are the simply hopes that we keep from some people or as future consequences, or are the our imaginative thoughts?, Are they are future goals or something that we made up to feel good?. I know a some of you will agree with me and a huge number of my readers will also deny my perceptions. But think for yourself… what are your wishes? What made you think that way? Why are you wishing what you are wishing for? Aren't your wishes trying to make you be what you are not?, Draupadi wished for a husband who was intelligent, humble, strongest of all, known of all the scriptures and one who is the greatest of all warriors, but little did she knew what she is wishing for is not possible for one man to have and rest is history…Questions are countless and the answers to them varies as per your wishes and the choices you make in life...

A Small Wish

There's a simple wish I have
I wish to make my wishes come true
In number which are very few.…

I wish to make my mother proud,
So she may feel
That the seed that she sowed has started to sprout…

I wish to make my sister happy,
Coz she is so dear to me and a bit crazy…

I wish to make my dreams come true
I wish to wake on a day so new
Where there is nothing but opportunities
New life, new challenges, new duties

I wish to wish more someday
The wish of a day with no sorrow, no gay,
I wish that day comes soon
With a bright sun and a full moon……

12. Weird Nature of People

Now here's something we all will relate to, people and their weird nature. There are so many instances when people choose to behave a per their choices with others unknown to the fact as of what they are making the other person feel. You act according to your situations and people respond according to there's and that's when conflicts start developing. It is very important for each one of us to understand every other being, not all shoes are meant for all of us to fit in, people are different and so are their perceptions towards every different situations. What one thinks to be six, someone might think it to be nine, none of them is wrong but their perception differs and that makes all the difference.

<u>Weird Nature of People</u>

I wonder time passes so fast
All that seemed near
Becomes a matter of past
And that's what we start to fear…

Something that seems soo good today
May become dangerous tomorrow,
Something that today gives us worry & gay..

May tomorrow lead us to happiness and no sorrow….

People too change with time,
Sometimes it's necessary, can't be considered a crime,
They may change for their benefit or others..
Those who change for themselves
Never consider other's important neither they bother..

Those who change for others
They treat everyone like their brother's n sisters

Very few people change in such a manner,
They face criticisms and wars
They don't care how high the critics rise,
All that matters is the passion to sacrifice..

13. Another Wish

I sometimes feel wishes are also weird like some people's nature. Like sometimes we wish for things which are next to impossible, for example, sometimes I wish to fly like birds up and high with no restrictions no boundaries, but we all know it costs a lot to actually experience that…However, not all wishes are expensive some are completely in our hands, like I wish to be happy. I wish to be successful, I wish to become a teacher or any other professional title it can be. Your wishes define you, reflect your personality and help you grow as a person, or for instance a better person. No matter what our wishes are, they motivate us to strive and work hard for their fulfilment and make impossible, possible.

Another Wish

Hours pass me sitting
Keeping quiet and dreaming
Thinking of my dream and its worries
The achievements and sorries..

I wish, my career dream comes true
As my wishes are not too large, they are few…
I wish, I get to do what I wish to…

As I wish to go for something new…

I can't imagine my dream's broken
Can't let my passion rotten
I am desperate to begin a new life, to face realities
A life of new challenges and opportunities

I pray everyday to god that
May my wishes come true
So that I can climb the success ladder
And far I may fly on that mat
May happiness stand for me & my family in a queue

I wish my dreams are fulfilled
Although they are nothing until I wake up…
I wish I could go through everything with my mind chilled,
And with anger & loss, I may make up….

14. Love

As we talked earlier, the most used and misused words are *I Love You,* but digging deep, do the people using these words actually mean them?, or do they actually know the real meaning of love?

Have you ever passed a phase where you realised, that who are the people in your life, that actually love you, for me it was when I realised it was my 'Family'. The unconditional love of family is incomparable. The love your mother has towards you, the pamper and affection bestowed by your father, the protection you are surrounded by, by your elder brother/sister and the innocence of your younger sibling, all are beyond words can ever explain…

Love

The most unconditional love in the world
Is the love of a mother
She loves her child with no complaints
When we are in pain
With sadness she faints…..

The care of a father too is so lovely,
He protects us always

No matter our path is of two feet's or infinity…..

There's nothing that these people demand from us..
Hence their RESPECT is must..
The only thing they expect from their child,
Is a life where they may see him surrounded with
happiness….

We are lucky to have parents and a family…
A mother so sweet,
A father so strong,,
A sister…..a twin soul..
Its all that matter to have..
Every happiness is there, that gets in them a bit roll……

15. Wishes

'Wishes'…Oxford Languages dictionary defines 'Wishes' as : 'to feel or express a strong desire or fope for something that cannot or probably will not happen.' This definition makes me feel so depressed, my wishes have always been my ray of hope, they have been my inspiration to always move ahead and wish for more, Why settle for less, when you can wish and achieve more. My genuine condolences to people who think wishes are something that cannot happen, look at mine…

I Wish

I just wish I could achieve what I want
I wish I can live my dream

a dream that's not so old
a dream that's not too new
that shines in my eyes like a gold
and people knowing it are few

I wish I could be called a poetess one day
may people know my mother by my title's name
the day with glory and no gay
that's full of happiness and fame

I wish people to love my work
I wish them to appreciate
I wish to be taught for my mistakes
I wish to be admired for the one's I didn't do.....

I just wish I could achieve what I want
I wish I can live my dream
I wish to see my asleep dream come true...
the one that now didn't let me sleep......

16. Distances

"The scariest thing about distance is that you don't know whether they'll miss you or forget you."

— Nicholas Sparks, The Notebook

Distances… so aptly said by Nicholas Sparks, distances are the most unpredictable, you never know, whether someone distant from you will miss you or they will eventually forget you, however, distances always teach you a lot. They are our most under-rated tutors. When we are in continuous contact with someone, we tend to see what they want us to see, but when they are distant from us we tend to move towards them with our perception and that's when we start exploring their true colours… Distances are amazing, they are painful, they are true, they are harsh, they are more than what we can just about…

Distances

Distances ARE SO Weird
They are NOT Something TO BE Feared
They Usually Teach US A Lesson
They Build A NEW YOU
Brings A NEW Passion

IT Teaches THE Importance OF Someone Dear
Which WE Usually NOT Feel When They ARE Near

Distances Have Both Positive AND Negative Aspects
Effects OF Which Never Ends

WE Miss FEW People When Distances Increases
WE Even Miss FEW When Distances Decrease..
FEW People Seems TO BE Good AT A Distance
BUT When They ARE Near They Change AT AN Instance
Although, Distances From FEW People Hurts TOO Much
Even Though THE Number OF Such People IS NOT TOO
Much

Distances ARE THE Best Mirrors
TOO View Everyone's Actual Image..
AND TO Bring Ourselves OUT OF A Misunderstanding
Cage....

This is a work that completely dwelled out of my imaginations, but it gave me infinite words to express my abstract ideas. And if even a single word connected with your soul or made you think twice about your own feelings, your wishes, your guilts or your surrounding... I Won.

www.ingramcontent.com/pod-product-compliance
Lightning Source LLC
Chambersburg PA
CBHW060230170726
48004CB00004BA/1502